HOLID

D1000684

J 973.1 SHOW ES
COLUMBUS DAY ·
4.50 BRONX RESERVE

3 3333 03987 4645

FD

The New York Public Library

Astor, Lenox and Tilden Foundations

FD

The Branch Libraries
FORDHAM LIBRARY CENTER
2556 Bainbridge Avenue
Bronx, N.Y. 10458

Books may be returned to any branch of
The New York Public Library. Non-print
media must be returned to the branch from
which borrowed.

Materials must be returned by last date
stamped on card. Fines are charged for
overdue items.

Form #0415

Columbus Day

A CROWELL HOLIDAY BOOK

Columbus Day

By Paul Showers • Illustrations by Ed Emberley

Thomas Y. Crowell Company, New York

CROWELL HOLIDAY BOOKS

Edited by Susan Bartlett Weber

Copyright © 1965 by Paul Showers. Illustrations copyright © 1965 by Ed Emberley. All rights reserved. No part of this book may be reproduced in any form, except by a reviewer, without the permission of the publisher. Manufactured in the United States of America. Library of Congress Catalog Card No. 65-16186   2 3 4 5 6 7 8 9 10

J 973.1
S

J750121

EX—

Columbus Day

Every day ships with big white sails came from faraway places to the city of Genoa in Italy. A boy named Christopher sometimes stood on the pier, with the wind blowing in his hair and the gray gulls flying overhead, and watched the ships. He liked to watch the sailors as they worked, and when they sailed away again, it made him sad to see them wave goodbye. He wanted to go with them.

Christopher's father was a weaver. He had a shop in Genoa where he made cloth on looms. Christopher worked in the shop, but he didn't like weaving nearly as much as he liked the sea.

In a few years Christopher was old enough to get a job on a ship. Then he began making long trips to faraway ports. By the time he was a man he had become a very good sailor. He was not afraid of danger and he knew how to handle a ship in all kinds of weather. He left Genoa and went to live in the city of Lisbon in Portugal. Merchants hired him to be the captain of their ships and to go on long voyages. Now he was called by his full name — Christopher Columbus.

In those days many merchants traveled to China, Japan and India. They called these countries the Indies. There they bought gold, pearls, spices and fine silk cloth.

It was a long and dangerous journey to the Indies. There were robbers and wild animals along the way. The merchants went in caravans over high mountains and hot deserts. Always they went east toward the rising sun.

Columbus wanted to go to the Indies, too, but he thought there was a better way to get there. He had read many books and had studied maps. He knew the world was round.

If you can go east around the world and reach the Indies, why can't you go west around the world and reach them too, he asked. It would be easy to sail west across the ocean toward the setting sun. It would be quicker, too, he thought.

Columbus gathered up his books and maps and went to see the King of Portugal. He explained his plan and asked the King to help him buy some ships. The King called in his wise men. They listened to Columbus and looked at his maps. Then they shook their heads. Nobody had ever done such a thing before, they said.

Next Columbus went to see the King and Queen of Spain. Again he brought out his books and maps and begged the King and Queen to help him. At last they agreed that Columbus might be right, and they gave him money to pay for three ships and to hire men to sail them.

The ships were the *Santa Maria,* the *Nina* and the *Pinta.* They were small, but they were sturdy and fast. In September Columbus started to sail west across the ocean. It was the year 1492. No one on board the three little ships knew what was ahead, for none of them had ever sailed that way before. But Columbus said this was the way to go to the Indies. And everybody hoped he was right.

The sun shone brightly and the sea was calm. The ships raced along smoothly in a steady wind. Day after day went by. A week passed. Then a second week. And a third.

The sailors could see nothing but water. Land was far behind them. Little by little they began to be afraid. None of them had ever been so far from land before. They grumbled. They said they had gone far enough and that it was time to turn around. But Columbus would not turn back.

Some of the men began to talk secretly among themselves. They wanted to push Columbus overboard. They could say he had slipped and had fallen into the sea. Then they could turn the ships around and head for home.

Columbus knew the men were against him, but he kept sailing west. He was sure he would find land. He scolded the men for grumbling. Then he cheered them up by talking about the gold and the pearls they would find when they reached the Indies.

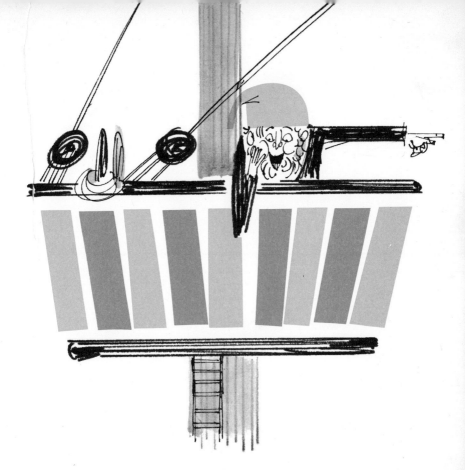

Every day the sailors kept watch. One evening as the sun was setting one of the men thought he saw land. Everybody shouted for joy. Even Columbus kneeled on deck and said a prayer of thanks. But it was not land. It was only some low clouds in the distance.

The birds helped the men keep up their courage. Almost every day, sea birds flew over the ships. Whenever the sailors saw them, they felt better. They were sure land could not be far away if there were birds.

The last day of September, which was Sunday, eight birds flew over. On Monday and Tuesday they saw more birds. But on Wednesday they counted only a few. The

sailors were afraid they had been near an island and had passed by. They begged Columbus to turn back, but he would not. He kept on sailing west.

Another day passed and another. The food and water were almost gone. On October 7 there was a great shout and everybody rushed to look. Again a sailor thought he saw land ahead. But again it was only clouds. The men were more frightened than ever.

Then a wonderful thing happened. Suddenly out of the sky from the north came thousands of birds. They were strange birds with many different colors and markings. All day they passed over the ships in great flocks.

Columbus watched them carefully. They made him think of the little birds that sang in the fields back home. They were land birds and they were flying to the southwest.

That day for the first time the ships changed direction. They turned from the west to the southwest. Columbus had decided to follow the birds.

That night he and his men got little sleep. They watched the sea ahead. There was a bright moon and against it they could see the flying birds. But the next morning there was no land in sight, only waves stretching to the horizon. Some of the birds settled down on the ship to rest.

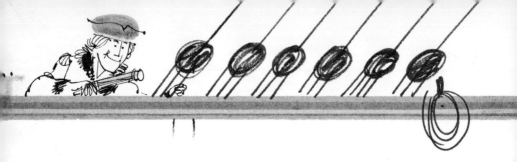

When another dawn came and there was still no sign of land, the men grew angry. They had not seen trees or grass for more than a month. It was a dangerous time for Columbus. There was nothing he could say to cheer up the men.

On October 11, a branch with green leaves floated past the *Santa Maria.* Then the men on the *Nina* saw a branch with red berries on it.

That night Columbus stood watch on the deck. About 10 o'clock he thought he saw a light ahead. An excited sailor thought he saw the light, too, but it disappeared and the ships sailed on in the dark.

Early the next morning there was a shout from a sailor on the *Pinta*. Land! Land ahead! The captain of the *Pinta* fired off a gun as a signal.

This time it was no false alarm. As the sun rose, the sailors saw an island before them with white sandy beaches and green forests. It was the morning of October 12.

Under a clear blue sky, the ships dropped their anchors and Columbus and his men rowed to shore in small boats. With them they took the flag of the King and Queen of Spain. They also took a white flag with a green cross. It belonged to Columbus because he was the head of the expedition.

When they reached the shore, some of the men fell down and kissed the ground. Then they kneeled with Columbus and said a prayer of thanks.

That day Columbus thought he had reached one of the islands of the Indies. He found people there who had dark skins like the people of the Indies. He called them Indians and they have been called Indians ever since. Columbus thought that China was not far away and started to look for it.

He found more islands with more dark-skinned people. On one of the islands they brought him gold. Then he was sure he had reached the Indies. He sailed back to Spain, taking some Indians with him to prove what he had found.

When he reached the Spanish court, the King and Queen rose from their thrones to greet him. It was a great day for Columbus. Everybody thought he had found a new way to reach the Indies.

After that Columbus made three more voyages west across the ocean. On each trip he found more islands and each time he was sure he would find China.

But Columbus had made a mistake. He had not found the islands of the Indies near China. They were still thousands of miles to the west. He had found the islands that lie between North and South America. Only nobody knew there were such places as North and South America. They didn't even have names yet.

Once Columbus landed on the shore of South America, but he thought it was only another island. He sailed on because he was still looking for China. He spent the rest of his life looking for it, but he never found it.

Columbus was disappointed because he did not find China. He did not know he had done something much more important. On October 12, 1492, he had found a part of the world that people knew nothing about — America. Now, on October 12, people honor and remember Columbus for what he did.

In the United States October 12 is called Columbus Day in some states and Discovery Day in others. People hang out flags and make speeches. Sometimes schools hold special programs about Columbus, with music and pageants. Sometimes there is no school at all.

In some cities there are parades. Los Angeles and San Francisco have parades; so does Boston. New York has a huge Columbus Day parade. On a bright, sunny day, it is a wonderful sight.

Thousands of people march up Fifth Avenue past Rockefeller Center and Central Park. All the shops hang out big flags, and crowds line the sidewalks to applaud the marchers as they pass.

School classes parade in their best dresses and suits. Boy Scout troops go by with flags and banners. There are fife and drum corps in bright uniforms, soldiers and sailors, and all kinds of bands. Everyone carries flags. On and on they march from morning until afternoon.

In South America October 12 is a holiday, too. In some cities people decorate the statues of Columbus with flowers.

Columbus is known by different names in different countries. In Portugal he is called Colom. In Spain and the countries of South America where people speak Spanish his name is Colón. The French know him as Colomb and the Italians call him Cristoforo Colombo.

But no matter how people say his name, October 12 is the day when they like to remember what he did. On that day they honor him — the brave man who would not give up.

About the Author

Paul Showers is a newspaperman and writer. He began as a copy editor on the Detroit *Free Press* and later worked on the New York *Herald Tribune*. He spent the war years in Japan, where he was a sergeant on the staff of *Yank,* the Army weekly. After a brief stint on the New York *Sunday Mirror,* he joined the staff of *The New York Times,* where he is now assistant travel editor.

Mr. Showers was born in Sunnyside, Washington. He received his B.A. from the University of Michigan. He now lives in suburban New Jersey with his family.

About the Illustrator

When he is not writing or illustrating, Ed Emberley pursues several interesting hobbies. He prints limited editions of children's books on his own hand press, studies Early Americana, and experiments with toy-making.

Mr. Emberley received a Bachelor of Fine Arts degree from the Massachusetts College of Art in Boston. He lives in Ipswich, Massachusetts, with his family.